Not Until You're Ready

DANYELLE SCROGGINS

S
PUBLISHING

Published by:
DIVINELY SOWN PUBLISHING
2715 Jewella Avenue
Shreveport, Louisiana 71130
http://www.danyellescroggins.com/d-s-publishing.html

ISBN-13: 978-0-9960038-8-9
ISBN-10: 0-9960038-8-6

Second Edition paperback November 2017
10 9 8 7 6 5 4 3 2 1

Printed in the United States of America

Book Design: Danyelle Scroggins

Exclusive discounts are available for quantity purchases. For details, contact the publisher at the address above.

This book is dedicated to my loving husband, Pastor Reynard C. Scroggins Sr. and to my children Raiyawna, Dobrielle, & Dwight Jr.

~~~~~~~~~~~~~~~~~~~~~~~~~~~~~~~

In Loving Memory of the late Sis. L.B. Ford, praying, faithful grandmother; Louis Ford, wonderful grandfather; Sup. David Gatlin Sr., a unique, honest, and excellent leader; Min. Linda Baldwin, spiritual mother & Pastor Arthur Washington, devoted pastor

These are the people who prayed me through, and although their journeys have ended, their legacy lives on; they are truly missed.

"He giveth power to the faint; and to them that have no might he increaseth strength. Even the youths shall faint and be weary, and the young men shall utterly fall: But they that wait upon the LORD shall renew their strength; they shall mount up with wings as eagles; they shall run, and not be weary; and they shall walk, and not faint. "

ISAIAH 40:29-31

Contents

Introduction

It is a known fact that there are women all over the world praying for God to intervene in their lives granting husbands to them according to the prayers that they have rendered unto Him. Altar calls at churches are filled with single women, some with their children and tears waiting for an all mighty intervention. They are confident after so many failed relationships that it is going to take something special to get that wonder-man they've been waiting for and some by faith is believing for just that. With so many things already against them like so many good men are already married, and a good man but has no financial stability.

Then there are these situations he's a good man has a great job but a homosexual, single with no intentions of getting married, and he prefers a woman with no children. Not to mention this... he seems to be a good man but does not attend church, or he is a good guy but not saved and does not know the Lord; it almost seems hopeless to ever find the mate they desire. I used the word find because most women feel like it is up to them to find the man they dream of having and of course, there is where the problems begin.

I too thought the same thing, and I know exactly what goes on in the minds of those in this situation. I have with much prayer and supplication deemed it necessary to share my ordeal with the entire world to get women back on the track that we should be on. I was one of these women, and with the help of the Lord, my life changed over a period of three years, and I pray that I can help you to see things the way God allowed me to see them.

My sisters and brothers who desire to know the move of God towards relationships read this book and be blessed.

With love,

Pastor Danyelle Scroggins

CHAPTER ONE

Find

That word find is indeed a word that causes most women to make their most significant mistakes. After an eight-year marriage, I came home with the words find and man in the same sentence and nearly destroyed my life. You know every woman feels that she is in control of her life and she also feels that her style of dressing and facial appearance makes up a significant proportion of the essence of who she is. So she most definitely thinks that she is in control of the type of men she attracts by her efforts, but unfortunately, this is not so.

The King James Version of the Bible states explicitly, "Whoso findeth a wife findeth a good thing and obtaineth favour of the Lord." Proverbs 18:22

This scripture alone should allow a woman to see that it is not her job to find a man. When God designed the woman, take notice that He did not have to tell Adam who Eve was.

Genesis 2:21-24 When God brought Eve to Adam, Adam said, "This is now bone of my bones, and flesh of my flesh:"

I used that to say, "A man knows his woman." Once he finds her, it will take an army to keep him from her. Women, the task of finding a mate is far beyond you. I pray that you are intelligent enough to realize that it is far better to wait to be found than to find. I was so bent on finding someone to love me until it clouded my mind and my judgment. I thought that the beauty God gave me (outer and inner) was a tool for helping. Please allow Proverbs 31:30 to soak into your spirit.

"Favor is deceitful, and beauty is vain: but a woman that feareth the Lord, she shall be praised."

It is not about how you look. That's why you'll find a not so attractive woman with a handsome man or vice versa. There is an indescribable beauty that comes from a woman that fears the Lord. Even though her facial features might not appear to be what you think it should be, her heart and the beauty of it are undeniable. I was so eager to find a man until I allowed the men I encountered to overcloud my good judgment, concerning what I knew was right. Oh, they would tell me how pretty I was. The next thing you know, I was going on dates, and then a couple of dates led to a couple of nightcaps and fornication became the highlight of the night.

I knew it was better to marry than to burn but it seemed I had to fornicate until I happened upon a husband. I want you to know that a lot of sisters get married so they can have sex. Sex is not a legitimate cause for marriage. You had better learned how to ask the Lord to help you to keep your flesh under subjection to His Spirit.

You would be surprised at the number of women who say that they married because they were trying to live holy but were having sexual relations. They figured because they enjoyed the sex they might as well marry the guy, and their marriages failed within months. The best relationships are the ones built on love and trust and not sex. Being a young woman, we say, "You got to test out the goods before you buy them." That is a lie from the pit of hell. If Satan can cloud your better judgment with propaganda and myths, then he can control your activities with the same thing. Sex is an integral part of marriage, but it's by far not the most important.

I was married at the age of seventeen and being that I married military, I moved to Yokosuka Japan where we lived for five years. There are many motives besides sex why women marry, but mine was because of pregnancy. Pregnant at the age of seventeen, I felt that it was good for me to marry so that I would not have to raise a child alone. I know you are wondering what a seventeen-year-old know about marriage, and I can assure you hardly anything. Times were sometimes rough, and the only thing that helped was that we both came from strong religious upbringings. He was from the Church of God in Christ, and I was Baptist. We both had sense enough to pray if nothing else. It was prayer that kept us together for as long as we were but it was our actions along with the help of family gatherings that drove us apart.

Neither one of us knew the life apart that awaited us but both of us, especially me, was willing to find out. After years of marriage and two more children, we got a divorce. Now at twenty-five, I had to learn how to become an even more responsible adult. No longer did I have to come in at a particular time or be a wife. I was now single and back living the life that I had let slip by me. Even if I didn't know how I was going to eat or where I was going to work, I knew that I could find me a man.

It was not as easy as I thought it would be. This is where I could give my ex-awards because he was a hard act to follow. He was a communicator, and you just do not find that in too many men. I was looking for a man who would talk and play UNO and board games because our lives were filled with excitement, but some men just did not talk. I asked for a divorce on July 3rd the day after my eighth anniversary, the divorce became final in March, and my ex-was married in June.

God had to reconstruct my thought pattern, and He knew exactly how He was going to do it. I cannot describe the pain I felt to know that my ex-husband was already remarried and I had not even gone on my first date for grieving. I was still trying to figure out where we went wrong and how to be fair with our children and he was now raising someone else's children. I felt that we should both heal and be repaired, but he could not stand the thought of being alone. He had always warned me that if I left him, he would find another wife and he did just that. So of course, this began the obsession of "The Find."

I was still going to church every Sunday like usual, and I felt as saved as I was before the divorce, but I was not. I was torn on the inside, and it seemed that not even God could repair my heart from the pain it suffered. After visiting a couple of churches, I finally found a Church of God in Christ that I felt suited me. The pastor was a young gentleman, who was very attractive, but this did not matter to me at all because I only wanted a pastor and not a lover. I did not even want a pastor to want to be a lover.

I had gone through being hit on by my pastor, and I did not like the way it left me feeling. I went into this ministry telling the pastor precisely what I did not want from him, and he became a friend or better yet a brother that was dear to me. I put this in because you would be surprised at the women drawn to their pastors. It's like he becomes a man you can lean on, and then you develop the wrong types of feelings. Not because you are attracted to him but the Spirit that resides in him. I thank God that Satan did not attack me concerning him with vile vain affections because at the time I needed someone who would give a precise word from the Lord, and he did just that.

He encouraged me, and in the midst of all of this, my grandmother died. So I was dealing with hurt on top of hurt, and unless you've been there, you wouldn't know the half of what I was feeling. I only wished his wife would have felt the same way about me. Although I was on the find quest, I respected him for who he was and her for being the best part of him. Being so vulnerable and so hurt from the past, just a whisper from the dark found a place within to hinder me from dealing with the rejection I felt. Because my state of mind was so fragile, (it could very well have been nothing except a lie that escalated into something), I left the ministry.

God had delivered me from a nasty attitude and some ridiculous ways, and to keep myself from acting a fool or idiot, I felt that it would be better for me to just leave. Even so, it had been the body of religion that my ex-husband had been born and raised in, and if I were to ever separate from him, I needed to separate from his religion but not our belief.

His church offered something that my church rarely spoke on, and I was convinced that it wasn't about the church it was about the believer. I would leave the church we attended but never the practice that his Dad had taught me throughout the years. His dad was a Superintendent in the church, and his total joy was in the Lord. He would sit down and teach me the word of God in between visits and I was just drawn to his knowledge of the Word and his determination to live the Word he taught. I was taught and now knew holiness was not only in the church organization, but it was in the real church...that believer who chose to give their all to God and live separate from the world.

Remember pastors' wife that just because a female has the goal of finding a man, does not mean she wants your man. Although there are those that the devil has selected to put in your ministry just to tempt him and to cause corruption, disruption, sin, and division, there could still be one that has chosen your ministry to get the help that God saw fit for your husband (and only your husband) to give. Try the spirit by the spirit. If she has not the spirit of the Living God, teach the young woman the way. This is your part in her life and in your husband's and your ministry.

I never truly realized how important it was for the older woman to teach the younger woman the way (Titus 2). But I also found out that though older has a lot to do with age, it also has a lot to do with experience. When you have been through some things, it's easier for you to have compassion on someone else going through. We must teach and instruct with compassion. Do not be ashamed of telling these youngsters where you have been and what you've been through. How will they know that God has delivered unless you let them know He has?

I pray that you embrace the fact that finding a mate is not up to you but it is entirely up to divine intervention by God Himself and shown to the man. God will allow you to be found, but it's only when you're ready. A few more headaches and a few more heartaches would cause me to see just that. With God, the lessons that are really meant for you to learn and live by seem to be the hardest lessons you'll ever learn. For me, this was one of them. I still insisted on finding my own husband, and I found myself in another devastating relationship. This time it was a married pastor, of a large church, in a different city but the same state as the one I lived in.

It is so easy for a person to say what they won't do if they are never faced with the challenge of doing it. I was a young female now working two jobs with a feeling a loneliness that ended my night and started my day. Facing everyday longing for someone in my life to love me and of course just as God knew my feelings, so did Satan. Satan will invade your thoughts and desires, and you must take control over the enemy. So often, we never realize the tricks of the enemy until we are deep in junk.

There I was working in a famous hotel, and prince charming (that was in town preaching a revival) handed me a tip that was larger than what I made in weeks pay. He provided an opportunity for me to quit one of my jobs and still have the financial assistance that I needed. He offered trips to where he lived and luxurious evenings in some of the most extravagant hotels in the city. I still knew God, went to church and knew that what I was doing was wrong but I felt like I had found him, my man.

Oh, how easy it is to be taken away by finances and popularity. I was living on his funds and relished in his notoriety. His friends knew me, and as I rode in limos and beautiful luxury cars, I felt like I was on top of the world. He and the Mrs. Lady would be on the seventh floor, and I'd be on the third floor. Where was the Holy Spirit? Why did God allow this to happen? God allows us to make our own decisions no matter who we are and what we are in Him.

He was speaking in all kinds of places, and I was in Bible College and speaking in different places but still no conviction. Well, not until I came home from a trip and my house was burglarized. Some of my most valuable possessions were stolen and just when I began to cry, the Holy Spirit brought to my attention something that I will never forget...

"Danyelle, you only feel exactly what his wife feels every time he walks out of the door...invaded. Thou shalt not steal."

Those words are some of the harshest words that the Spirit has ever uttered to me. Still, I ignored the warning just like we often do and went again only to have everything that he replaced stolen again. God did not have to warn me again. I finally got the message. Every time I was with this man, I was stealing! He was not my man, and no matter how many problems he claimed to have had in his marriage, he was still married. What was even worst, he was a man of God, and I was a woman of God, and neither one of us felt the embarrassment that we should have felt. It was only the grace of God that kept us alive, and we owe our lives to God. God saved us even when we were committing adultery on Him and on their marriage.

What an awesome God we serve! After the second time, I got the message and repented for my actions. I never went back to that city again not even to visit, and I did not owe him an explanation why. I just stopped everything. In the midst of falling in relationships, we had better remember that,

"The body is not for fornication but for the Lord; and the Lord for the body." (1 Corinthians 6:13) and "For this is the will of God, even your sanctification, that ye should abstain from fornication."(1 Thessalonians 4:3)

Depending on what type of relationships we fall in if it is a married person, we had better remember that "Marriage is honorable in all, and the bed undefiled: but whoremongers and adulterers God will judge." (Hebrews 13:4)

This friend is where finding a man can get you. Yes in situations you started out trying to prevent. It is so easy to get caught up in things you said that you would never get caught up in. Satan is awaiting a moment's breakdown in your relationship with God to impart into your soul filth. Don't allow him the authority to participate in your life's decisions. You must take full authority over your flesh by encouraging the spirit of the Living God that lives within to rule over your soul and your flesh. We must remember that the Spirit of God is placed within to keep us even when we are too weak to keep ourselves. I have since learned a new prayer... "Lord, please keep me even when I can't keep myself. For if you keep me, I'll remain kept." Amen.

See it is imperative that we realize that we need help being kept. God will keep you in all your ways. Acknowledge Him, and He will direct your path (Proverbs 3:6). God knows our hearts, and also the type of husband we need and desire. Wait on God because this is a life-changing relationship. Marriage is great when you are married to the mate God chose. It can be horrible when you are married to someone you found and gave an ultimatum.

I've noticed when women find a husband, it's usually that old marry me this year or else thing. When you've been found, he generally has marriage already in his mind. Remember, that when it's your time, it will happen. If you've been married once and now divorced, sit down and write all the lessons you learned from the first marriage. It wasn't just his fault you divorced. God allows us the golden opportunity to see where we went wrong. Unless you know how will you prevent it in the next marriage. Don't find yourself a mate....Prepare yourself to be found!

CHAPTER TWO

Loneliness

It was this feeling that helped me to land myself in the arms and bed of a married man. My God, how low we will go to cure this disease of the heart and mind that penetrates, too heavily, making us forget what matters the most. After this God spoke to me concerning loneliness...

"Danyelle don't you know that I am with you and I will never forsake you. I did not leave you comfortless, and I will come to you whenever you need me. You are a daughter to me, and I am a Father unto you. Wholeness and completeness come entirely from me, and I am able to give it to you just as I have given unto you life."

God is so wonderful. Even in the midst of your mess, He will speak to you with words of comfort. He allows you to see the full picture of your problem or injuries of sin so you can make a full recovery after repentance. He's just that kind of God, showing us our true selves to better ourselves.

As you can see, "The Find" was helping me to dig myself into a pit that was easy to get into but harder to come out of; "Loneliness" was keeping me in the dugout. This should have stopped me from digging, but of course, it did not. I found myself in two more relationships in the course of the two years after the divorce and left with two more scars; all for the sake of a cure for loneliness. So many women have found themselves in this place once or twice in their lives. You just have to remember that God is always with you.

It did not help me the fact that every man I dated was a minister. Automatically, they claimed that God sent them and I believed it. Every man you meet is not, I repeat, is not a blessing from the Lord!

Proverbs 10:22 says..."The blessing of the Lord, it maketh rich, and addeth no sorrow with it."

Anything that is considered a blessing that brings sorrow or sin is not from God.

Is He Faking and Shaking?

Just because a man is in the church and or preaching the Word of God does not mean that he has fully surrendered himself unto the Lord. Satan will use whoever allows himself to be used by him and it does not matter whether you are called of God or not. So many women feel like just because they meet a man in the church, he is saved and filled with the Holy Ghost. Wrong answer and conclusion!

You have some men confessing Christ but have yet to have experienced the baptism of the Holy Spirit. Women so often mistake a church attendee, or a church participator, to be the perfect man. Baby, Satan goes to church every Sunday. He is in the choir, on the usher board, on the deacon board, on the trustee board, and what is so heartbreaking, he is even in the pulpit.

Yes, there or some fakers and shakers or we can call them "imitators" in the church who preach for selfish gain (Read Philippians 1:12-18), and women include their gain. Satan has derived himself a plan to duplicate everything that God has ever made and to try to do it better, with no avail. He still falls short and will forever fall short. That's why it is so important for you to get this, "Beloved believe not every spirit but try the spirits whether they are of God" (1 John 4:1).

God will surely make you aware of who is real and who is not. You must also remember that the church is God's hospital. Many of men have been hurt by women who proclaimed to be of God but weren't. Just like you are going to church praying to be delivered from some things, he might just be doing the same thing. What are the chances of those two patients who have been told that they were going to die from cancer getting married? Although they relate to one another, they also don't want to cause the other any more pain than they already have.

They both figure what the use in getting married if, in fact, they don't have long to live. The same ought to apply to two sin infected persons. Why date a person in the church who is going through the same sickness of sin as you are, but have not fully recovered? You might be familiar with one another, but the familiarity could cause you both to slip back into the sin. Wouldn't it be so much better to be recovered fornicators? At least you both know the wages that follow the sin and its' devastating effects on a family, and you can go through rehabilitation every Sunday morning together? God will show you the heart of those who are approaching you, but you must hear and heed the warnings. All for the sake of having someone in their lives. Open your ears and HEAR! And once you have listened except what you hear and move on.

I used the word hear because sometimes it is with our ears that we are first made aware of someone's heart.

"A good man out of the good treasure of his heart bringeth forth that which is good, and an evil man out of the evil treasure of his heart bringeth forth that which is evil: for of the abundance of the heart his mouth speaketh." Luke 6:45

See, because we walk by faith and not by sight, and are not God, it is sometimes hard to see a man's internal corruption. God does not deal with our eyes, but He deals significantly with our ears. Satan, on the other hand, deals a lot with our eyes. Lust starts with the eyes, and many marriages are based on lust. God deals with the inner depths, and after you have heard, you believe, you change, and you grow in faith. Sometimes don't talk just listen.

Most of the time, a person will say something with their mouth that you will hear and it will do something to you on the inside. A lot of times because you don't want to believe what you heard, you try to make excuses for what was said or either pretend that you never heard it. Isn't it funny how God gives us warnings, but we ignore them? Oh, how we try so hard to ignore them if they aren't what we like or if they expose what we want.

I talk to a lot of women who knew their husbands cheated while they were dating and they marry in spite of and then he cheats in the marriage. I have met women who say that their spouse told them that they needed more than one woman before they married but then act as though it's a big surprise to find out he's cheating during the marriage. God gave warnings, and they didn't heed the warnings.

It is often what I hear a person say that allows me to know what to pray for. After I speak, if God uses me to tear down some of Satan's strongholds, people (after service) say things to me that I never would have imagined. Sometimes it is in the matter of minutes that I know their heart and if they are delivered or not.

So often it comes from people who I never would have imagined in a million of years would say these things. But nevertheless, it does. We must keep in mind that God will reveal things to us to keep us from getting hurt. That is just His way of protecting His children. So this leads me to believe that we had better watch what we say because what we say will reveal our personality and spirituality.

If you really want to know if a person is saved or if he truly knows the Lord, the best way to find these things out is to listen to what he or she has to say. Sometimes you can see a church members' feeling on working for God through their actions on Sunday mornings, but you can see their relationship with God by their conversation every other morning or day.

The Bible says, "...for it is out of the abundance of the heart, that the mouth speaks" (Luke 6:45). I only know what is deep in your heart when I listen to what you say. You had better hear people and stop allowing your mind to whitewash over what they say. I know, it's just easier to like them better if you believe you did not just hear what they said, but trust me, it is far better to embrace that what you've just heard and move forward.

It is one thing to work and another to have faith while you work. A person with faith-based works has a relationship with God that shows in their daily walk in this life. Pay attention to the conversations that you encounter!

Don't allow the spirit of loneliness to cause you to suffer more grief than you'll need. I am a firm believer that God allows us to go through some things to strengthen and build us. But I am also a firm believer that guided sense is better than bought sense any day. God is always there. I do believe that he created woman so that Adam would not be alone, but I also believe that he proved He was still with Adam in the garden when he spoke to them after they ate of the forbidden fruit. We must not allow the perception of loneliness to impose or infringe upon us the desire to partake in sin.

I too have been in a place in my life where it seemed that God had left me all by myself. I had to come to the realization that it was time for me to be still and stay firmly planted on the fact that God was there all along. His love is ever abounding, and someone who loves you will never leave you. God's love is so incredible, and if you just stand still and breathe, you'll see the provisions of His love in every breath.

CHAPTER THREE

When Enough Is Enough

After going through so much heartache added to the scars from a broken marriage, I finally felt like I had had enough. Yes, enough of being lied to and abused by unmerited relationships. That word "find" was no longer apart of my vocabulary about men. There is something about when we stop trying to fix things ourselves. See God can't speak to us or even use us to the fullest of our abilities when we have our own agendas. Sometimes He simply allows us to gather bumps and bruises, headaches and heartaches before He intervenes. We are so not capable of doing God's job but how we try so hard. I really got sick and tired of being sick and tired, and it was not until then that God really began to impart things into my spirit. They were things that would help me and help to bring other women out of the pits that we were in.

I was so deep in the pit of my sins: fornication, adultery, and lying until I fell in and couldn't even pull myself out even if I tried.

"Whosoever diggeth a pit shall fall therein:...." (Proverbs 26:27).

Not only was this pit full of my sins that I had taken along with me, it was full of the pain that I had experienced as a girl longing for the affection of her father. I was his only daughter and his only child that was claimed but yet in still, his alcoholic addiction caused him to break many promises, and I hated him for that. I also contained all the pain I felt when I found out that my ex-husband had cheated on me and all the sexual situations I had engaged in as a teenager but finally I was sick of being in the pit. It is a good thing when you get sick of sin. It is a bad thing that you allowed yourself to become so deep in it until you began to get sick of it. By one token people saw a new Danyelle because of the walk that they thought I had with God but they just didn't know that the old Danyelle was emerging and operating but being hidden.

God will allow your under-cover operations to be covered up while he gives warnings. Then, if you don't adhere to the warnings, He will pull the cover from over your undercover operations, or He will allow those lurking demonic spirits to tell your secrets, and that just isn't good. Have you ever seen someone in Christ that is known for good all over but after years of good something bad is brought out in the opening? Sometimes God would have sent warnings after warnings, for them to clean up their acts, but they just ignored the warnings. They were so caught up in themselves and their actions until they couldn't hear the voice of God bringing forth warnings.

"Pride goeth before destruction and a haughty spirit before a fall." (Proverbs 16:18)

I was tired of hiding. I was tired of hurting. I wanted nothing more than to be the woman God has chosen for me to be but I did not know how to be her. I decided that since I was approaching my third year of being divorced that it was now time to get it together. The kids wondered when was I going to get them a dad and for the first time, I knew that it was not up to me. I was not the husband finder or the Daddy finder, and I was not going to pretend anymore like I was. This was beyond me, and for the first time in my life, I knew that I had no control over the turnout or the outcome of the situation. It is so good to come to this point because this is when God does His best work.

When you have totally surrendered the situation to Him, He can do what He does best, and that is, fix things. Everywhere in the Holy Bible after the birth of Jesus, you find that His ministry was all about fixing people and their situations. But the most unique key to all of the fixing that Jesus did was when people were ready to surrender their situation unto Him, or either when they had nowhere else to turn. He asks questions like, "Wilt thou be made whole?"

It's one thing for people to see that you need fixing but it's another for you to recognize that you need it. I understand better the scripture that says if you confess your sins, God is faithful and just to forgive you and cleanse you from all unrighteousness. Confession is good for your soul and your mind. Satan can't beat you up with things that are already in the open. God is a forgiving God, and although He sees everything, your confession allows Him to show us His faithfulness. God desires to clean you from anything that hinders your purpose in this life, but you must first know that you need cleaning.

I was not sure how to regain me, but I knew that I was as low as low could be. I couldn't find any peace with going out to the clubs with the girls. I couldn't even find peace hanging out in the restaurants with friends. All I wanted to do was just wallow in the pity party that I had thrown for myself and relish in the pity that some of my friends shown to me. Everyone knew that I was going through something even though they didn't quite know precisely what it was. Was it a new transformation going on that would stand the test of time? Or was it the beginning of real life unknown? I really didn't have a clue but what I did know was that I was so low that I was face down on the floor of my destruction.

God put me on the floor on my face so that I might genuinely humble myself before Him. This is the start of my cleanup period. My face down on the dirty floor was a symbol of my lowest point and what was before me was the climb to being able to stand. Lots of tears, lots of prayers, lots of worship, and plenty of praises.

CHAPTER FOUR

Clean-Up Time

As I laid on the floor face down by night in prayer, I began to bury myself in the church by day. I hardly had time to breathe for seminary school, Sunday school, matron meetings, pastor aid department meetings, and anything else I could be involved in. Finally, I began to embrace 1 Corinthians 7:34...

"There is a difference also between a wife and a virgin. The unmarried woman careth for the things of the Lord that she may be holy both in body and in spirit:...."

See, I had to become so wrapped up in the things of the Lord that the things that I wanted and felt didn't matter. I started my days with Jesus, and I finished my nights with Jesus. God began to clean me up. By the time that I was able to roll over onto my back, I was able to receive some of the revelations of my life; I was finally able to see myself.

My pit desires began to vanish one by one. I no longer blamed my dad for me not being able to trust men or having to have a man. I no longer blamed my ex-husband for ruining my life and causing me to leave my family and friends. I no longer blamed him for allowing his family to help ruin our marriage. I no longer blamed a few of his family members for not loving me like I felt they should have. I no longer needed sex to feel loved or wanted.

I no longer needed the comfort of another woman's man, a man to cure my feelings of loneliness, because I no longer felt lonely. I no longer blamed my mother for my mishaps (allowing me to be grown). God began to break down loneliness, and He uncovered it as the lie that Satan has conjured up to get His women caught up in the snares or sin. All that mattered at the end of the day was that I had begun or completed a task that would be pleasing to God and would help to upbuild His kingdom.

More and more I got stronger and stronger. I began to recognize Satan for who he was and the part he had played in my life to separate me from the love of God. And believe me, just because I was here now, does not mean that men stop flirting. Baby, I had more men hollering at me than I had ever had in my entire life. They were handsome, rich, educated, smart, loving, kind, leaders, and tall. Everything I ever thought I wanted in a man came after me. Satan knew exactly what I liked, and he enticed me with the best of the best. They drove nice luxury cars, they had nice jobs, spoke of good intentions, and said they loved the Lord, but because God loved me, God sustained me.

It seems like at my weakest moments, He would give me a task or send me out on assignments that allowed me to encourage other women to be strong and at the same time, He was giving to me strength. Then is when I really learned that I could do all things through Christ for He strengthens me. I began to come in the house and just lie down on the floor and worship God for who He was. I gained an overwhelming sense of worship as He cleaned me up from the inside out.

I really did not totally realize just how dirty and polluted I was until God began to clean me. You know so many times we ask God to clean us and as soon as we think we are cleaned we stop asking. My friend, it is a daily thing that we should pray for, and if you are not praying for God to clean you up, you need to be praying that He keep you clean. God showed me that we were just like toilets, no matter how clean we look or how cleaned we smelled we are still considered to be a dirty object.

No matter how clean your toilet is, you still would not want to drink from it. That's just how we are, but the good thing is that God has made us to be flushed of our impurities, just like a toilet and after we've flushed by repenting, He puts it in a sea of forgetfulness never to remember it again. It is so easy to be polluted with the pollution of this world, but it is so hard to become cleansed from it. Our carnal man absorbs things of the world like a sponge absorbs water and it infiltrates our Spiritual man. We must be aware of the wickedness of this world.

As I laid on my face, God began with my heart..."Danyelle, your heart has cart webs in it. Although you called yourself cleaning things out of your heart, you didn't." At the time I lived in a brick house with wood under the car porch. Every time I would go out and sweep the cart webs from the ceiling, in a matter of days, they would come right back.

God said to me, "Your heart is exactly like the car porch. Every time you have tried to get rid of the hurtful things, in a matter of days they came right back. You had many temporary fixes to some permanent problems and situations and you never fully allowed me to clean them up. Danyelle, if you just allow me to completely clean the cart webs out of your heart, you will never have to deal with some of the things you've dwelt with again."

These words were like music to my ears. I finally knew why every time I felt like I had gotten over the divorce, I realized I hadn't and why every time I tried to really get a relationship with my dad, I failed. I had not allowed God to clean my heart. After He imparted this into my spirit, I changed my prayer to...God clean the cart webs out of my heart completely restoring it with love and your word. I found myself asking God to give me His heart and still to this day I ask God to give me His heart. In this Christian walk, it is imperative that your heart is right. If your heart is not right, you will do and say anything. Not to mention you will act any kind of way and live anyway.

Scriptures for the Heart

David said in **Psalm 51:10**

"Create in me a clean heart, O God; and renew a right spirit within me."

The writer of **Psalm 119:80** ask the Lord

"Let my heart be sound in thy statutes; that I be not ashamed."

The writer of **Psalm 119:11** says

"Thy word have I hid in mine heart, that I might not sin against thee."

I used these three because they best suited my situation and me. I needed God to remove the filth and replace it with His word and His statues so that I could walk in the way according to Salvation. So many times people go into marriages with everything but the right things in their hearts. It is hard to operate in love with a corrupt heart. It is so not strange when I see couples that have only been married for a few months getting divorces because they say that the love is gone.

They failed to realize that love was not there in the first place. I can remember when I married for the first time. I was only seventeen, and the man I married was not the man I felt I truly loved. I thought I was so in love with a guy I meet when I was five years old and just knew that I would marry.

34

I felt that obligation and responsibilities made me fall in love with my ex-husband but if there is one thing I know now; I know that love never fails. If you love someone and truly love him or her, somewhere deep in your heart they remain. God has a way of making that love that you once felt for a person stain your memory but then become brotherly love. When you forgive that person, you'll find that for the rest of your life you will care about that person.

Over the years I developed a brotherly love for my ex-husband and for the rest of our lives we share children that belong to the both of us, reminding us of the family unit we betrayed and it can't be taken away. Before you can fully allow your heart to love someone, it must be cleansed and purged from things and people that don't belong.

Love is a beautiful thing, and we were founded by love. Christ loved us so much that He was willing and willingly gave His life for us. His love is, so heartfelt and so genuine, and although He has given us the purest and simplest example of what love really is, we still fail to know and give love. Our love is so conditional, and as long as you do for me, what I feel like you ought to be doing, I love you. It is based upon the conditions that surround our relationship, and this is not what or how God intended for our love to be.

Satan fights so hard against love because it is contained in the two greatest commands. (Mark 12:30-31)

"Thou shalt love the Lord thy God with all thy heart, and with all thy soul, and with all thy mind, and with all thy strength: this is the first commandment."

"And the second is like, namely this, Thou shalt love thy neighbour as thyself. There is none other commandment greater than these."

See, if Satan can keep you from loving, he can keep you from heaven. Love never fails. Marriages do, but love doesn't. And I must break down what we call the reasons for divorces. We often say that if he or she is committing adultery, that is the number one reason for divorce. Tell me, how often have you committed adultery on Jesus? How many times have you done it knowingly and willingly?

How many times have you disappointed God or neglected to do His will? How many vows have you broken that you made to Him? We know that God is a jealous God but that never stops us from making our jobs, our home, our spouses, our money, our children, our church, our pastor, or our feelings little gods in our lives. But how many times do we run to God after He's brought our actions to the forefront of our attention and say, "I'm sorry"? And how many times does He forgive us?

There is no excuse for divorce. So now that you know, this repent sincerely for the divorce and stop making excuses for it and believe that God will forgive. It's all a part of the cleanup. Cleaning up the things that caused

you to walk in unforgiveness. Or even the things that
caused you not to love.

CHAPTER FIVE

What You Don't Know About Sex

During this year of purification, God began to share with me what really happens during sex. You know when God himself gives you a revelation it will almost blow you away because of its profoundness. He knew that the simplest way of me understanding and retaining what He had to tell me, was to show me.

First, He took me back into my own life concerning that guy that I was in love with since age five. During my teenage years, he became the first guy that I had ever had sex with. Although he was supposed to be my boyfriend he had other girlfriends. I would catch him in stores with other women, and he would lie out of it. It never really dune on me how attached I was to this guy until I got married and moved away.

Coming home was good because I missed my family, but it was bad because I missed him. I was a married woman with a child who I just knew was his, so that did not make things any better. This made coming home a bad nightmare. My husband hated him. Because of my husband's insecurity of me and this guy's sexual relationship with one another, he had sex outside of the marriage. That, of course, became the key to me being able to be with this guy and feel no remorse. See, one bad situation leads to another bad situation. My husband probably never would have looked at another woman if he were secure. The lack of security in a relationship will cause people to do things that they would not ordinarily do.

He begged me to leave my husband, and we start a life together and even though this is what I wanted I just couldn't bring myself to doing this. I remembered all the times it was supposed to be just him and me and another woman would always pop up. I also remembered how my husband had taken me away from him because he was part of the reason why I married in the first place. I often asked God why it was so hard to stop loving him and why I just couldn't forget and it was not until after I was divorced and now, that He decided to give me the answer.

Our bodies were created only be shared with our husband and him alone. Because we are made of body, spirit, and soul, they each play a part in the sexual process. Once we share our bodies through sexual intercourse with a man or vice versa, our soul, which houses our affections and our emotions, embraces this person to be our spouses and there becomes the beginning of what is called soul ties. Our spirit then interprets this to be a spiritual union before God, and you began to share things that are of the spirit with this person. Remember that marriage is a spiritual connection.

That is why it is so hard to get rid of a person whom you have shared sexual intercourse with. You know you see women as well as men being physically and emotionally abused by a mate but still they hold on to a relationship that you feel like they should have gotten rid of. This is why. They are spiritually tied to this person, and it is not as easy as you think it is to be rid of them. And in the process, their spirit man became filled and intertwined with this person as if it were a marriage. If anyone of you has ever been married and divorce, you know that marriage is easier to get in than it is to get out.

Sometimes a person goes through pure hell before they get out of a relationship and some of them never make it because they are murdered. Soul ties are real, and all of the time a person never loses the ties until they pray in deep sincerity for God to remove that person from their hearts.

Once God revealed this to me, I was able to get cleansed from all of the spirits within. It does not matter how many persons you have had sex with, each time you pick up something. Whether it is something good or bad, you become the carrier of the trait. Those evil spirits can be so life-altering until when you finally take a good look at yourself, you really don't have a clue of whom you are.

Demonic spirits can cause you to do and say some things that you were not accustomed to, and when you are in sin, there is no such way of protecting yourself from being accessible to their reign. The sharing of your body goes more in-depth than your mind can even fathom.

When you find a married couple, you find one person. The Bible says "...and the two shall become one." It takes one body, one soul, and one spirit to make one person so then, how do two people become one? God takes two bodies in marriage and conjoins a spiritual link between two souls to form "one."

In the course of writing this book, a friend of mine, who's an older lady, (I will go as far to call her a spiritual guidance for me) shared something with me. She and her husband had been married for years and had six children together, but he died. She said after his death she was lost. It was as if she had to get to know herself all over again. She said some days she couldn't think or remember and because of the concern that she was losing her mind, she sought the wisdom of a friend who was older than she. This friend explained to her that with her husband she was a whole. Now she was used to functioning as a whole, she would now have to wait on God to make the half, a complete, with oneness with Him.

Is not that the best thing you have ever heard? That is why a husband can finish the sentences of his wife and how wives know their husband's thoughts before they even think them. That is also why some people after they have lost their spouses die just weeks or months later. They are so used to being a whole until they can't even fathom the thought of being by themselves, and their grief becomes so overwhelming until it kills them.

It is very important that you realize that there is a reason for the warnings against fornication. When your

41

body is free from the sin of fornication and all of the demonic spirits that comes along with this sin, God can use you. Sexual sins take so much out of you. They cause you to believe that what you are doing is natural. Our bodies are made to desire sex because of reproduction. God wouldn't have given us these desires unless they were apart of His plan to replenish the Earth.

Sex is for two married adults so that they may reproduce and raise Godly offsprings. Remember the story of Noah, God gave Noah precise instructions to take two animals male and female as the same with his sons that took their wives. Look how important sex was in the rebuilding of a nation after the flood. We must not take sex as a casual got to get it event. Abstain! I rebuke every lustful spirit that has caused you to use your body as someone else's pleasure piece. I come against every sexual connotation that has you bound. In the name of Jesus. Amen.

Scriptures on Fornication

"...Now the body is not for fornication, but for the Lord; and the Lord for the body." 1 Corinthians 6:13

"Flee fornication. Every sin that a man doeth is without the body; but he that commiteth fornications sinneth against his own body. What? Know ye not that your body is the temple of the Holy Ghost which is in you, which ye have of God, and ye are not your own? For ye are bought with a price: therefore glorify God in your body, and in your spirit, which are God's." 1 Corinthians 6:18-20

"I say therefore to the unmarried and widows, It is good for them if they abide even as I. But if they cannot contain, let them marry: for it is better to marry than to burn." 1 Corinthians 7:8-9

"For this is the will of God, even your sanctification, that ye should abstain from fornication:" 1 Thessalonians 4:3

"The Lord knoweth how to deliver the godly out of temptations, and to reserve the unjust unto the day of judgment to be punished:" 2 Peter 2:9

"For in that he himself hath suffered being tempted, he is able to succour them that are tempted." Hebrews 2:18

God desires to have your body as a house to hold His Spirit.

Questions to really think about....

Will you present your body as a living sacrifice? Will you give God your all? Will you remember to be spiritually led instead of emotionally led?

CHAPTER SIX

Doing What's Right, Not Determined by Age

Being only in my twenties, it was really hard for me not having a boyfriend; not having all the pleasures that came along with having one, like it is for some of you. I knew the Lord, and I knew that sex was wrong, but I was still engaging in it. Most women in their twenties are just beginning to experiences sex and the perks that come along with it, like a boyfriend being the number one perk. Most girls in her twenties feel as if she is not complete without a partner but this, too, is a lie from the pit of hell.

You are so complete with Jesus, and you don't even know this because you haven't yet given your whole heart to Him. Most women know Him because of their parents or grandparents but they never really know Him until they experience some heart-felt situations on their own. You don't have to be in a relationship with a man to get what you are longing for at this age. Most of the time, it is as simple as just wanting someone to talk too.

Talk to Jesus, and I promise He will talk to you. Some just need something as simple as for someone to love them and who better to love you than Jesus himself. You must always keep on the center point of your mind...

John 3:16..."For God so loved the world, that he gave his only begotten Son, that whosever believeth in him should not perish, but have everlasting life."

This is one that I hold at the center-point of my mind and in the corners of my heart, John 15:13..."Greater love hath no man than this that a man lay down his life for his friends."

Everything that you are looking for is in Jesus. You don't have to wait until you are in your forties or fifties to know the Lord. Oh, how much more fulfilling your life would be if only you embraced Him in your youth; when you are able to do so much more for Him. Sometimes, God will show you how your soul is being damned to hell to deliver you from your sins. This that He showed me changed my entire life. I began to ask God to teach me how to bring my body under subjection to His will and His ways. I pleaded with God to cleanse me of all the spirits that I had picked up through sexual sins over the course of my life. I know this seems unreal coming from a thirty-four-year-old female, but God is powerful enough to meet you at the age and circumstance that you are at and fix you for His service. I finally after this was really not concerned about finding or wanting a husband.

God knew that I was not ready, just like you. He allows us to go through. Our going through is not to break us, His children, but for us to see our faults and learn from them. Punishment or should I say the storm for me was being without a mate. I was so used to having someone to talk to in the middle of the night. I was used to just having someone there. I had my stepdad when I was young living at home, and when I left my parent's house, I went to the home of my husband. I had never experienced living alone without a man, and the fear that associated itself with my present situation allowed me to do some stupid stuff. If I can help young women and girls by passing some of the pain and agony that I had to go through to keep them from going through, I would have really done something on this side of life.

You would be so amazed at how God can use you to do some things you never would have imagined doing. I am still young, and I have never been happier. I finally have my priorities in line. It was a long time coming, but I'm there. I just want to encourage other young women to just give their lives to the Lord fully and completely, committed and dedicated to Him for His services and you will be happier than you have ever been in your entire life.

Don't let your financial situations over-shadow what you really need. When you are young and trying to make it on your own, it is hard. You are often tempted by the assistance of someone who wants nothing more than to get something in return. If you've ever been here before it doesn't matter how many bills they pay, you still are broke. Satan tries to persuade you into believing that he's there to help you but in all actuality, Satan has sent him to harm you. Even though it is not physical or emotional, you better believe it is spiritual. Be careful young women. All help is not good help. But God's help exceeds good.

I run into so many young women in the wrong types of relationships, but they seem to refuse to be in a solid relationship with God. Instead of searching for the wrong things....try searching for a solid relationship with your Creator. The word says that if you knock the doors will be open. That means, if you seek God, you will find Him. You'll find Him is the simplest things like the smiles on people's faces or even the voice that speaks to you in the quietness of the day. He is there, and He is waiting for you. My grandmother used to say, "Why not give God your whole heart now?" She's in heaven with the Lord, but the question still floats in my mind.... why did I wait so long to give Him my whole heart?

Don't let your youth rob you of spending time and getting to know the Lord. I often watch how my girls react in church and to certain things. I have taught them that if they give God their all now why they are young, God will return the gesture. My girls are eighteen and fifteen, and they are both virgins. This doesn't mean that I still don't have to fight in the spirit for their flesh. I refuse to allow the enemy to feel that he can have any parts of their lives and it starts now. I teach vigorously that there is a place for unsaved sinners called Hell.

I also teach them that they have the freedom of choice. Choose you this day who you will serve. My kids understand that you can't serve yourself and God at the same time.

CHAPTER SEVEN

Are You Really Ready

There are so many things that God desires for you. Trust me, He is not going to give them until you are ready. You must remember that God knows the heart and just because you say that you won't change for the worst if He gives you what you desire, He knows exactly how you are going to react.

For example:

You've been praying for a financial blessing. You are living by God's commandments, and you don't mind bringing your tithes into the storehouse so that it might bring meat into His house, but still no financial blessing. Your plans are as soon as you get the blessing to pay your tithes and then pay some other bills and give a couple of people at least a hundred dollars. Nevertheless, God knows from Him being all-knowing and Him knowing your heart that you are going to do nothing that you said you were. He knows that you'll only give half of what you were supposed to pay in tithes and He knows that you will only probably bless two persons with fifty dollars instead of one hundred. So the moral of the story is you can't fool God. No matter what your intentions are, He knows exactly what your actions will be.

Another example:

You've been asking God for a husband. Well, you say that when God gives you that husband that you will not change. You will still be going to bible study and all of your other church functions, and you will also still be engaging in your wife duties like you are suppose to. Well God knows that even though you said that is what you were going to do, you won't. He knows that you will use your church duties to get out of cleaning the house. He also knows that you will even probably never cook a meal for this hard working man because you claim to be so deep in study.

See once we realize that God knows, we won't make false premeditated vows of what we are going to do. In turn, we will just ask God to prepare us to handle the blessings that He has in store for us so that we won't put nothing before Him, turn against Him, or become unfaithful to Him or our duties. So sometimes you have to really ask yourself the question, "Am I really ready to receive the blessing that I have asked God for?" You will know the answer as soon as you ask the question.

If by chance that you find out that you are not ready, ask God to prepare you to receive the blessing that you have prayed for. There is nothing wrong about asking God to prepare you for what He has in store for you. He knows that everything takes preparation. The example of His life shows a period of preparation.

I can remember when I first got into the ministry. I was so eager to just preach the Gospel. I knew only a few scriptures, and to me, that was all that I needed to preach, a few scriptures. I thought that I was prepared to teach a multitude and God said, "No." I was then moved to another church that absolutely did not allow even the thought of women in ministry. I could not understand for the life of me why God would send me to this church if He had called me to the ministry.

Well, some males that are operating out of self might say that the reason I was sent there is so that I could know that women aren't supposed to be in ministry but what the devil might have meant for my bad, God meant it for my good. I was able to teach Sunday school, and president a women's mission society that prepared me for witnessing and public speaking. I took part in an early morning teachers meeting (under the same preacher that didn't believe in women in ministry) in which I was taught about the different dispensations and in full the book of Genesis. Meanwhile, in Bible College, I was studying the book of Revelation. God was teaching me the beginning while teaching me the end! See these are the two books that Satan fights so hard against because one tells his beginning and the other his end.

Isn't God Good?

He used the very person who was against me being who I was to enhance who I was going to become. This was my preparation period, and even though sometimes I questioned God as to what He was doing in my life, He knew all the time. I couldn't see it, or I would not have believed it even if it had been revealed to me, but now that it was over I praised God for it. Although I thought that I was ready, I found out that I was not really prepared. I was not at all equipped for the tricks of the devil, and I had nothing really to fight with.

My knowledge of His word was so minute, and He knew He could not send me on the battlefield without full knowledge of how to fight the battle. Understand, that is why the military train their soldiers so hard and so much before sending them to battle. God does the same intense training for the soldiers that are on His battlefield. Nevertheless, those of us in the Lord's army understand fully that the battle is not ours, but it's the Lord's. He equips us to move at His command! He instructs us on our armor so that we will know how each piece is to be used in the warfare in which we fight. So the next time before you ask for something of God, ask yourself if you are ready to receive it. I would really hate for you to end up like me.

One night, at home in my bed, I was studying "The Life Of Christ" by Dr. Weldon Adams. He made the statement concerning the transfiguration of Jesus before the three disciples (paraphrasing) that unbelievers can't even imagine the Shekinah. It is a mystery that clouds their unbelieving minds, but to the believer, it is his strength and hope. This made me feel like I thank God for knowing, so I said out loud, "Lord show me your Shekinah glory." Before I could do anything, something happened. A light shone so bright and so quick in my eyes that I had to cover them with both of my hands to hide and tears began to roll down my cheeks like buckets of water were in my eyes.

The Lord allowed me to see a glimpse of His glory and it was so profound that I could not even stand to see it. When I finally uncovered my eyes, I looked at my husband who watched me in awe and said to him that I have to be careful what I ask God for. This left me on a high for the remaining of the night, and it was even hard for me to sleep without the tears. God will give you some of the things you ask for even though He knows you are unaware of the consequences of what you asked. I would have never in a million of years thought on this particular night, at this specific time, God would grant me whatever I uttered out of my mouth. Even though I have experienced a lot of things, they were nothing like what I experienced then.

Then just when I was prepared to tell Gods' word, there was another stumbling block. More men began to voice their opinions over the pulpit about women in ministry. Boy did it hurt so badly when they got up there and said, "God ain't called a woman." How could this be happening to me? I studied daily to find leading ladies of the Bible, and I needed to be able to counteract them when they came to me with this mess directly, I thought!

The Holy Spirit spoke to me after a lock-in situation and said, "The Word was made flesh and dwelt among women just like He dwelt among men. Did the Word not talk to women or tell women to go and give messages from Him? Well if the Word gave women messages then to give to the disciples and others, why then will the Word by His Spirit not give women messages now? Danyelle, you don't have to fight to prove who or what I have made you because no man knows my mind. For the gifts and the calling of God bestowed unto you are irrevocable."

Yes, another mind-blowing revelation. After this, I was ready to give God's word. It did not matter if they called me a minister or a missionary, a sister or an evangelist, a Sunday school teacher or an administrator...I did not care. It didn't matter if I couldn't speak behind the pulpit and it didn't even matter that I had to speak from the floor. None of that mess mattered at all. If it was going to coat their egos for me to stand like a wretched at the back door that would have been fine. Even if they would not have let me come in their churches that too would have been fine. Jesus came that He might save the loss and I can assure you that there are more loss folks at grocery stores and big wholesale stores than there are in the church.

This was just another trick of the devil started or brought about to bring separation and confusion amongst Gods' chosen people. We know that a house divided cannot stand and when you are God's child you are a part of His household. There are some women who God is calling for

53

in these last and evil days to spread the gospel, but you will not succeed in this until you are ready. Prepare yourself for the kingdom of God is at hand and the harvest is plenteous.

You surely don't have to wait until you are half past old to work for the Lord. There is a lady named Maxine Owens who I have great respect for. She is a member of Assembly Baptist Church, and most importantly she is a volunteer Chaplain for LSU and has been for several of years. She told me of how she began her work for the Lord at the age of twenty-eight and how she wished she would have started sooner. Now to me, that was young, but to her, it wasn't young enough. After the death of two children, and her parents, she tells of how she hungers to do so much more for the Lord. Is that not the best story you've ever heard? This work is longing work that you hunger and thirst after and with age the hunger gets more vibrant. She says, "Danyelle, I only wish that more women your age would hunger after Christ, His words, and to live a life like Christ."

This is where self-examination is vitally important. Before you go before God with requests, be sure that what you are requesting is what you are ready to receive. It is just like a kid...you know they just ate and are not at all hungry but the child is now asking for a peanut butter and jelly sandwich. Do you give it knowing that the child just finished a full course meal or do you remind the child that they just ate and wait until they are really ready to eat again? See sometimes God has to evaluate our requests

54

and determine if we are prepared to receive them or not. Sometimes we suffer from a case of greediness that we don't even realize we have. Sometimes it's a case of envy; we want just because someone else has it. So examine yourself and make sure that what you want from God is what God wants for you. Does your desire fit in His will for your life? It's that simple.

CHAPTER EIGHT

Only When You're Ready

It took three months of complete and total separation unto the Lord. It started with me praying on my stomach and then being able to roll over on my back. Then I was able to get on my knees, and after weeks on my knees, I was able to stand up on my own using the word of God as a foundation and His spoken words to me as rails for balancing. God began to open doors for me that were closed. School became so understandable, and the more I studied, the more I longed to know. The guys in school began to recognize me as an equal. Not just a lady who was in the wrong place in search for the wrong profession but as a fellow laborer whose words was just as important as theirs. Work began to not mean the same for me. God had already spoken to me before year one on my stomach was over telling me that it was time to leave the shop.

I had been a beautician since I graduated from high school and the money was good. I did not want to leave and was not going too until I went on a trip. I was with a young man who I use to date and felt the need to win him to Christ. My money was low, and he promised to help me buy the kids for Christmas if I would go with him. All the way I used John P Kee gospel cd to minister to him, and I sang until I felt it was sinking in. On the way back, we were pulled over by the police. They found out that there were seventeen pounds of marijuana in the back of the jeep. We were then taken to Henderson County Jail, and somehow instead of putting me in a holding cell, I was put in a library.

There was one book that stood out amongst all of the books there, and it was "John, On the Isle of Patmos." I did not have any intentions on reading this book, but the longer I sat there; the more this book screamed my name. When I read it, I was almost blown away. A cold book room became a warm, safe haven for God to speak through one book. It was then that I realized that I was special to Him and my reasons for being there was beyond the drugs and the guy. When they finally escorted me to the cell, it had about ten women already in it. It was cold there because they were having problems with the heat. My first words to the ladies were, "Don't stop talking now I need to hear all the noise that I could." So they started back up with the conversation, and I laid on the floor in front of the television.

I knew my parents did not have money to bail me out and my mother was already a wreck because my little brother was serving two years in Monroe. I could not dare break her heart because after all, I was her only child going to church and kept ragging on her about going. I specifically told God that I was waiting on Him to get me out of this mess. Finally, I drifted off to sleep and was awaken by a shadow sitting by my head. When I got up, there was a young lady sitting at the table, and she was waiting for me to wake up. She said, "Tell me, how I know when I am saved?"

The first thing I did was asked her how did she know to ask me and she responded by saying to me that "something" told her that I would know." You know, I knew that it was the Holy Spirit and I knew that He had already equipped me with the answers. I asked for a bible and was handed three. I took her to Romans 10:9 "That if thou shalt confess with thou mouth the Lord Jesus, and shalt believe in thine heart that God has raised Him from the dead, thou shalt be saved."

By the time I finished talking to the young lady, I had the attention of eight other young women. That Saturday night before bed I was asked to lead them in prayer and boy did the Spirit of God sweep through the cell. There were tears and clapping as well as some heartfelt Amen after the prayer. On Sunday evening, a missionary from one of the local churches came, and God allowed her to confirm everything that I had ministered unto them the night before. What a mighty God we served? How He sent a young lady of the same belief and faith as my own to utter the same words as myself.

On Sunday night, they wanted to have church, and that is what I did. I taught a couple of praise songs, and we had an entire service. At the closing of the worship period, I prayed, and I asked God to open the doors and allow freedom. Not only from this jail but also from the demons that controlled their lives. On Monday morning,

God began doing a work. They were calling women left and right to go the court. The very one who would not get involved was one of the ones who went home on that very night. Even in her unbelief, God managed to change her heart at the very end.

I came into the situation scared, but after reading the book, I knew that there was a divine purpose for my being there. God spoke to me and told me to call one of my friends who was the pastor in a small town in Texas to let him know where I was. He was concerned, but I assured him that I was all right. That Monday I found out that one of my cellmates first name was Danyelle and another one last name was Gatlin, which was my name at the time. I knew even more so that God intended for me to be there. Monday night when I laid down about seven o'clock, God asked me a question. He said, "Danyelle if I needed you to stay here, would you stay?" I answered from the depths of my heart when I said, "Lord, I don't want to stay but if you need me too, I will." One lonely tear dropped from the corner of my left eye, and it was only about three minutes later when I got a call on the intercom to pack my things because my seven hundred and fifty dollar bail had been paid.

I had no idea of who paid it, but I knew one thing, and that was God was in the midst. At the very same time, the young man who I was with had been bailed out and told the bail bond people that I was his girl and he was coming to get me out as soon as he went home and got his money. Boy, did I get four lessons at once...Trust and depend only on God. If a man/ woman is going to accept Christ, it will most certainly be by his own hearts conviction, and there was nothing I could do about it. My faith determines how quick or long I will go through any given situation, and that sometimes I am going to suffer some things for Christ sake.

The pastor from Texas bailed me out and said that the Lord told him to come and get me and even though he did not have the money, God told him exactly where to get it from. I will forever be grateful for his obedience to the voice of God. When I came home, I worked four more days in the beauty salon to pay the owner for the past week's booth rent and that week's rent, and I resigned!

I knew that this was a test of my faith and that to be the whole person I needed to be, I needed to leave the past behind. See while God has you on your face, back, and knees in prayer, you are going to go through some faith building seminars. Some might be easy whereas others might be hard but you must remain focus and keep in the corners of your mind Romans 8:28..."And we know that all things work together for good to those who love God, to them who are the called according to His purpose."

No matter what anyone thinks, I know that I had to go through this ordeal to gain some things that were so beneficial to my walk and relationship with God and because when God is in a situation, you will come out as pure gold. There is nowhere in my records that show that I have been in jail and people would not know unless they heard my testimony. Isn't that how God works? He throws sins in a sea of forgetfulness never to remember them again! Hallelujah!

After leaving the shop, I really became even the more dedicated at church. I had nothing to do but work for the Lord. I know you're wondering how I supported myself during this period and all I can say is, "God did it!" My lights were on six months without being paid, and when I did get a call that on Tuesday they would be shutting them off, my income tax check came in the mail that Monday. Baby, trust God and lean on Him and not what you know or what you think you know. People began giving me money and everywhere I went to speak, they gave me love offerings. I was being blessed beyond measures.

I was ready to receive from God, and He had opened the windows from heaven and was pouring on me like never before. I was baptized with the Holy Spirit, and I was given a song in another language that was the most beautiful song that I had ever heard. I was being blessed, and everyone saw it. One Sunday my ex-pastor was on to preach at another church and asked me if I were going. I avoided the question by running off when another member began to talk to him.

This time I really had no intentions on going. Just as my best friend and I got in her car with our kids to leave the church, he pulled up behind us and told us that he would pay for our gas to go. As you can see, we had no choice. The church was in Grand Cane, Louisiana and the pastor of that church and I were friends from far back. After service, he called me to the front where he and my

God-dad were talking, and I walked up telling him that it was about time that he got rid of those pop-bottled glasses he wore. He laughed and then told me that he was going to get his deacon to escort me out of his church. When the young man came over to where we were, his pastor gave him my hand. My God-dad asked the guy if he had a job and after the guy said, "yes," he gave the guy my other hand, and they started performing a marriage ceremony. Of course, we laughed, and I said, "Wait until we get to know each other before you marry us."

How powerful are your words spoken at God's altar because I found out that mine are powerful especially when on God's sacred ground and in a church filled with God's anointing. That day, I met my husband, and we never spent a day apart after our meeting on that Sunday. We met on September the 17th, and we married the following year on March the 17th and have now been married for seven years. My husband was a Holy Spirit filled deacon, and now he is an anointed, appointed, Holy Spirit filled Pastor preaching God's gospel.

God got me ready to be the wife of his own servant and layman. During the three-year period, God shared this with me... "Danyelle, I only have a few good men who want to serve me in spirit and in truth wholeheartedly. I have millions of women all over the world standing at altars praying for me to send them a man. If I gave one of my few good men to the woman who is not yet ready, one filled with the baggage of sin (and a sinful past that she has not yet dealt with), she is going to make him hate the day I ever allowed him to find her. He will no longer trust Me like he does and will not worship Me as I desire."

Boy, how that made so much sense to me. God desires that we are found, but because of our state of being, He won't allow that so we won't corrupt what is good and pleasing in His sight.

God says, "Women, for it is not until you're ready that I will open up my windows from heaven a pour you out blessings that you won't have room to receive. I know what you long for, and I know your every desire, I even know how some of you labor for me and how you are faithful to those things. I have told you to be faithful over a few things, and you will become ruler over many, but you have yet to give me your whole hearts, and when you do, I will reward you so that the whole world can see, but it is *Not Until You're Ready.*

About the Author

Danyelle L. Scroggins was born, raised, and reared in Shreveport, Louisiana. She attended the Greater Hope Baptist Church and the Mt. Nebo Baptist Church as a child. She is the wife of Pastor Reynard C. Scroggins and the mother of three children: Raiyawna, Dobrielle, and Dwight Gatlin Jr.; two stepsons Reynard & Gabriel Scroggins, and a granddaughter, Emiya'rai Grace.

Danyelle Scroggins currently serves as the Pastor of New Vessels Ministries North in Shreveport, Louisiana. She studied Theology at Louisiana Baptist University, has a Psychology Degree from the University of Phoenix, an Interdisciplinary Degree in Psychology /Biblical Studies from Liberty University, and a Master's in Religious Education from the Liberty University.

To find out more about Danyelle the author and pastor, visit her online at www.danyellescroggins.com.

EXCERPT FROM

Processed For Purpose

CHAPTER 1

I have been blessed in so many ways but understanding even when things are going unfavorable in my life, I'm still blessed, was indeed the area where I needed growth. You know, it's easy to believe you are blessed when things are going well, but when things are not so good, we often neglect the reality we are still blessed. Things can happen in your life suddenly, and when these things happen, you must remember they are not meant to devastate you to the point of no return.

I have a little secret...anytime something happens suddenly in my life, I always know God is somewhere in the program, and He's up to something. Remember in Acts when suddenly came a mighty rushing wind (Acts 2:2), I believe God uses the winds of circumstance to change the projection of our lives, suddenly. I think when we are humble, we look at things differently and when life changes suddenly, we are able to withstand knowing our trust is in God. Well, it took a while for me to get it.

My Marriage Beginnings

When I met my husband, he was a hardworking man who had been on the same job for over nineteen years. He was making a pretty good salary and took care of his family well. My attraction to my husband was based neither upon his job nor upon his ability to make money, but instead, I was attracted to his humility. I could not quite fathom how a man could be so humble, even to the point that nothing bothered him. When you are in church, one often experiences their fair share of stuff that should or could bother them but not my husband.

I would say, "Scroggins you just let people walk all over you," and his reply would always be, "You cannot walk over me and not be stopped by my God and if you walk over me, you have to pass by my God and be given permission by Him." He angered me because his confidence in the fact no one could do anything to him no matter whom they were, especially, if God was still with him or except God allowed was far beyond my mental capacity. My feeble mental mind said, "you do me in, I'm gonna find a way to do you in," and this made for a stressful life. Wow! How I envied my husband. I realized I wanted the assurance and humility Scroggins had.

There were times I tried to fake as if things did not bother me but my pride always got in the way. I never wanted folks to feel like they were playing me but Scroggins (with this different type of way), seemed to come out on top even when folks thought they were

66

doing him in. I wanted what he had but the one thing I had to learn is being humble or gaining humility would take process. No one just wakes up and decides today I am going to be humble. I wished it were this easy because had it been so, I would have just tried to fake it until I made it, knowing well that anything fake can never take on realness just because it looks the same or acts the same. (I want you to remember this and look at Isaiah 29:13.)

We can get there and be real, but it requires God's assistance. God is an all-knowing God, and He is as strategic as He is intentional. He knows when we desire humility because He knows when we get to a point when we are ready to stop struggling with what, who we are, to be what, and who He has ordained us to be. Therefore, God uses what I call processes to help us gain humility.

It was not that my husband became the apple of my eye because he was so good, it was that he was gifted. Gifted people stand out even in their way of thinking, and those of us who may be gifted in other areas can understand this. When you are gifted, your thought pattern is different and most gifted people, who know their gifts came from God, are humble. Now I am neither blind nor stupid, I have run into many folks who are gifted and proud. You would be surprised at gifted Christians who are full of pride. The very ones who are commanded to live a life of humility cannot deal with humanity because they are full of an epidemic called "Me." It's all about me, I'm doing me,

I'm living for me, and so goes and grows the epidemic which leads to self-righteousness and self-rightness (my word).

When a man believes he operates in his gifting because it is so naturally him or believes he owns it, he sometimes opts to make himself a gift. In other words, if you find a man full of pride, you will see a man who made himself a gift and never separated himself from his gifting. Or one who took the gifting from God as an attribute or characteristic of simply being him. Nonetheless, they need to remember the gift is from God and their character helps them to embrace the gift and operate accordingly. 1 Peter 4:10 says, "As each one has received a special gift, employ it in serving one another as good stewards of the manifold grace of God."

Now here is where we need a good glimpse of the Word of God...

"And whoever exalts himself will be humbled, and he who humbles himself will be exalted." Matthew 23:12

God blesses us with gifts not so that we can exalt ourselves or make ourselves look good to the world, which hates us, but instead, He gifts us so that we can aid one another in the kingdom and show forth His grace through our lives, so that He may be glorified.

When I first began preaching, it was difficult for a woman to go up into a church's pulpit because some of our brethren were not in agreement with women preaching the Gospel. The late Pastor Authur Washington whom I loved dearly for his humility said to me, "Daughter, look at Luke 14 with me, Jesus teaches on the lowly place so whenever you go into a sanctuary never go to their pulpit. It's better for them to ask you up than to ask you down." At that time, I was so angry. Having been treated bad, I figured so-called godly men rather I am a whoremonger than a preacher because as long as I had whoredom in my veins, preachers stayed in my face...but as soon as I turned from my wicked ways, they despised my gift of exhortation. I thank God for the late Pastor Washington because this lesson was a part of my process.

That is why it is hard to find me in the good girl preacher clicks. I do not need a click or connections to validate my calling or my gifts. All I need is the gift God has given me, enough character to operate inside of my gifting and outside of myself, and humility to walk in the calling and operate my gifting- God's way. I also believe as Andrew Wilson that there are no New Testament prohibitions on women preaching the gospel. I found out when I was about twelve years old God gifted me, and I had no choice whether or not I'd use the gift because my gifting has eluded to purpose, and where there is purpose, you become a target. Not just for people but for the enemy and the enemy in the inner you.

That may have startled you but sometimes gifted people start leaning on the gift instead of the giver, and they become complacent and arrogant in everything they do. See, humility makes you strive to bless the gift giver. I'm not concerned whether man accepts me, I'm concerned that I don't get lazy because of my gifting. I must study to show myself approved, I can never treat the giver of the gifting like a pimp, and that I always understand He (The Giver) could have chosen anyone else other than me to give my gift to. I work hard to stay close to The Giver because He and I together are more than the world for or against me.

This is where so many women are missing the mark. They feel like if they build a coalition with one another, then they can be accepted, but you have to know when God calls you, He validates you, and your gifting equips you. His acceptance of you is more than enough, and if you humble yourself, He will cause you to intertwine with Kings and Queens. I can remember when I first began to get engagements. Sometimes I would pray to get there and then when I get there, preach my heart out, I'd get this we cannot pay you speech and a basket of trinkets to add to the collection already in my kitchen drawer. Yes, I began to feel a certain type of way until God reminded me... you are my vessel, chosen by me, to do the work I have begun. If they never give you a dime, you be humble enough to except what they gave as the blessing they desire to receive.

Other Titles Brought to You by
DIVINELY SOWN PUBLISHING

Non-Fiction Titles:

Title:

40 Days of Healing

ISBN:

978-1-548067755

Title:

Processed for Purpose

ISBN:

978-0-996003865

Fiction Titles:

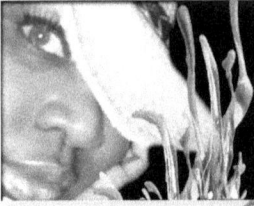
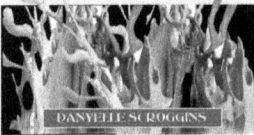

Title:

Put It in Ink

ISBN:

978-0-996003872

Title:

The Power of Pain, Restoration, Love, & Forgiving

ISBN:

978-0-996003858

Title:

Destiny's Decision

ISBN:

978-0996003810

www.ingramcontent.com/pod-product-compliance
Lightning Source LLC
Chambersburg PA
CBHW052218090426
42741CB00010B/2590